SPACE

JERRY WELLINGTON

Wayland

CONTENTS

4 Space

6 Views of the universe

8 Star gazing

10 Star patterns and galaxies

12 Our star – the Sun

14 Our moon and others

16 Satellites around the Earth

18 Rockets, shuttles, space stations

First published in 1995 by
Wayland (Publishers) Limited
61 Western Road, Hove, East
Sussex BN3 1JD, England
© Copyright 1995 Wayland
(Publishers) Ltd

British Library Cataloguing in
Publication Data
Wellington, Jerry
Space. – (Science Discovery
Series)
I. Title II. Series
523.1

ISBN 0 7502 1274 8

This book was prepared for
Wayland (Publishers) Limited by
Globe Education
of Nantwich, Cheshire

Concept David Jefferis
Illustrations Peter Bull

Printed and bound in Italy by
G. Canale and C.S.p.A., Turin

Acknowledgements
*Bridgeman Art Library 12;
Genesis/NASA 20, 21, 22/23, 23;
Science Photo Library cover (tl, centre, br, back), 6t, 6b, 8, 9, 10, 11t, 11b, 13t, 13b, 14, 16 17t 17b, 22, 24, 26t 26b, 27t, 27b, 28, 29, 30, 31t, 31b, 32–33t, 32–33b, 34, 35t, 35b, 36r 36–37, 37r, 38, 39, 40, 42, 43, 44, 46;
Tony Stone 4, 5, 8–9, 36l, 39;
Zefa 45.*

Planetary data tablulated on pages 23 and 24 was taken from Universe by William Kaufmann (W H Freeman, New York, 1994)

20	Travel to the moon and back	36	The Earth in space
22	The inner planets	38	Is there life out there?
24	The outer planets	40	The life and death of stars
26	Comets and shooting stars	42	Timeline of advance
28	Space travel – up and down	44	Glossary/1
30	Adapting to life in space	46	Glossary/2
32	Keeping clean and healthy	47	Going further
34	Eating and drinking	48	Index

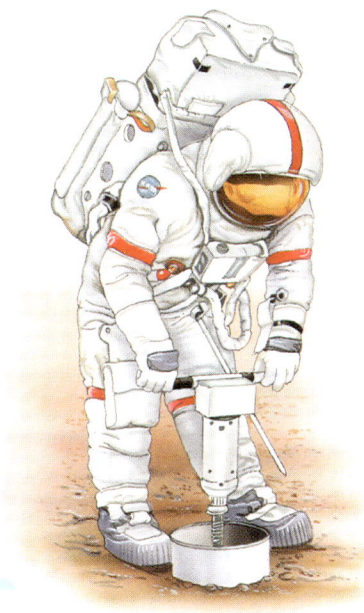

SPACE

You may have stared into space many a time. You may even have been told to stop doing it. But you were possibly thinking: what is space? where does it start? what lies out in space beyond the moon and the planets? how big is the universe and how old is it? when did it all begin and how? These are questions which have fascinated scientists, explorers and indeed most human beings for thousands of years.

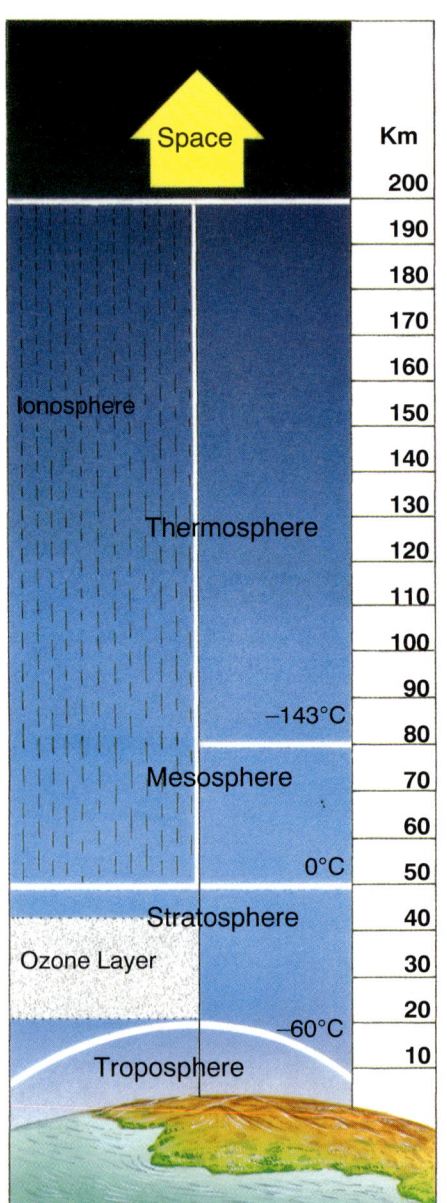

◀ The atmosphere around the Earth has several quite different layers. The layer nearest to the Earth is the troposphere. Here the temperature drops to about −60°C with increasing height but then rises again in the next layer, the stratosphere, to about 0°C. In the mesosphere it drops again to −143°C and then rises rapidly in the thermosphere.

The planet we all live on – planet Earth – is surrounded by a layer of gas that we call air. This is the Earth's atmosphere. The atmosphere is made up of a mixture of different gases: oxygen, nitrogen, and carbon dioxide are the main gases along with water vapour. This is the mixture of gases that allows us to live.

When you look into the sky by day you often see the water vapour in the atmosphere – especially in places which have plenty of rain. You might see fog and mist but if you are lucky you might see beautiful cloud formations.

Clouds form in the part of the atmosphere near the Earth's surface, in the layer called the troposphere. The peaks of the world's tallest mountains stretch high into the troposphere.

◀ **Clouds form when air cools and becomes saturated with water vapour. About half of the world is covered by cloud at any one time but only about 5 per cent of clouds produce rain.**

▼ **The Himalayas, on the border between Tibet and Nepal, contain some of the highest mountains in the world. Mount Everest was first climbed in 1953 by the New Zealand mountineer, Edmund Hillary, and the Sherpa, Tenzing Norgay. They wore masks and air tanks for the final climb to the summit. The picture below shows the view from the top of Everest towards Mount Makalu.**

Imagine you are riding up through the atmosphere in a special balloon. If you could rise above Mount Everest (about 9,000 metres high) the air would start to seem very thin. There would be so little oxygen that you would need breathing apparatus. Gradually, you rise into the next layer of the Earth's atmosphere – the stratosphere.

Now you have reached the region where jet aircraft fly. Keep rising in your imaginary balloon and you will reach the ozone layer. This is a part of the stratosphere, stretching upwards for about twenty kilometres, where the atmosphere contains molecules of a special gas called ozone. Ozone is special because it is made up of three oxygen atoms and helps to protect life on Earth from the harmful parts of the Sun's rays, the high energy ultraviolet rays.

Eventually, there is so little air that you have travelled beyond the Earth's atmosphere. You will have gone a distance similar to that between London and Paris (about 300 kilometres) but you are high enough to be in space. In space there is no air to keep us alive, only specks of dust and occasional clouds of gas. The water and oxygen that we need have been left far behind on Earth.

VIEWS OF THE UNIVERSE

The Egyptian astronomer and geographer Ptolemy (Claudius Ptolemaeus, about AD 90–168) suggested that the Earth was right at the middle of our universe and that the planets, the Sun and the other stars all travelled in orbit around it.

People believed in Ptolemy's ideas for many hundreds of years. These ideas fitted with their religious beliefs about the Earth, human beings and God, and it took a very brave Polish astronomer called Nicolaus Copernicus (1473–1543) to say that they were wrong. He suggested that the Earth and the planets orbit around the Sun.

▲ Nicolaus Copernicus developed a full mathematical model for his view of the universe. He published his ideas in 1543 (the year he died) in a book titled *The Revolution of the Heavenly Spheres*. This book, which was banned by the Catholic Church from 1616 until 1835, is now considered to be one of the first truly scientific works.

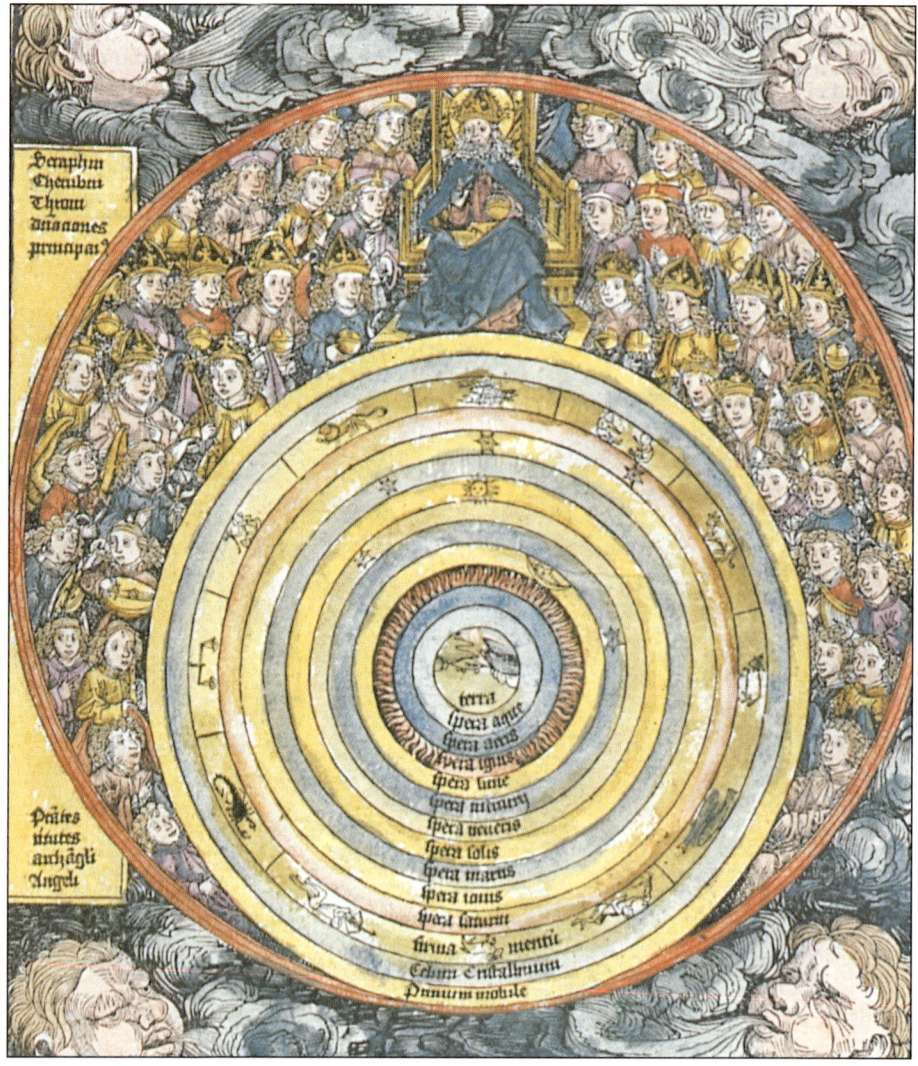

▶ An engraving dating from 1493 which illustrates Ptolemy's theory of the universe. The Earth is at the centre surrounded by spheres of water, air and fire. Outer spheres contain the moon; the planets Mercury, Venus, Mars, Jupiter and Saturn; the Sun and the stars. Watching over the universe are God and the nine classes of angels.

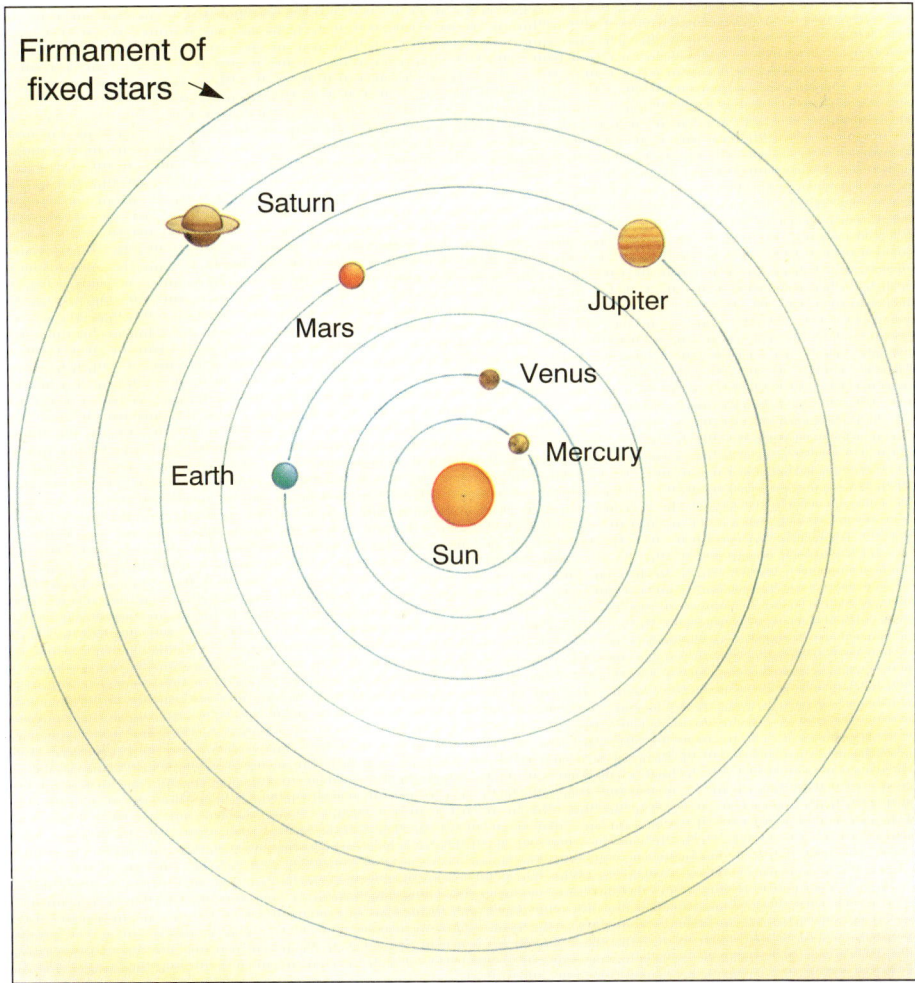

◀ **Copernicus suggested that the Sun was at the centre of the universe and that the planets moved round it in circular orbits.**

In the seventeenth century, the famous Italian astronomer Galileo Galilei (1564–1642) agreed with the Copernican model of the universe. Galileo was one of the first people to make use of a telescope to scan the heavens. His observations of space led him to say, '*Copernicus was right – the Sun is at the centre of the solar system, not the Earth.*' His ideas shocked the leaders of the Roman Catholic Church who, in 1633, confined him to his house for the rest of his life. The Church did not forgive him publicly until 1980, but he was long dead by then.

Views and beliefs about the universe have changed throughout the centuries and are likely to change again. This happens as scientists are able to make more and more observations of space and the universe with better and better tools and instruments. The old telescopes used by astronomers like Galileo and the English scientist Isaac Newton (1642–1726) were small and very basic compared with the exploring devices scientists have available today.

☀ THE BIG BANG

Many people today believe that the universe came into existence about 15,000 million years ago with a huge bang – it is called the big bang theory of the universe. Ever since the big bang, the universe has been expanding. The Earth, the solar system, the stars and the galaxies were all formed as a result of the big bang.

The big bang theory was first suggested in 1927 by Abbé Georges Lemaître in France and separately by Alexandra Friedmann in Russia. It is accepted by most scientists, but there are many other beliefs and theories about the universe, often depending on a person's religious or scientific background. This is an artist's impression of the way the big bang looked.

STAR GAZING

All through the centuries people have gazed into space. Long ago, the Chinese made careful records of events taking place in the night sky and we still have use of these records today. People believed that by studying the movements of the stars and planets, they could predict what would happen on Earth. This is the art of astrology. Astrology was taken very seriously by political and religious leaders until towards the end of the seventeenth century when the scientific revolution swept such superstitions aside.

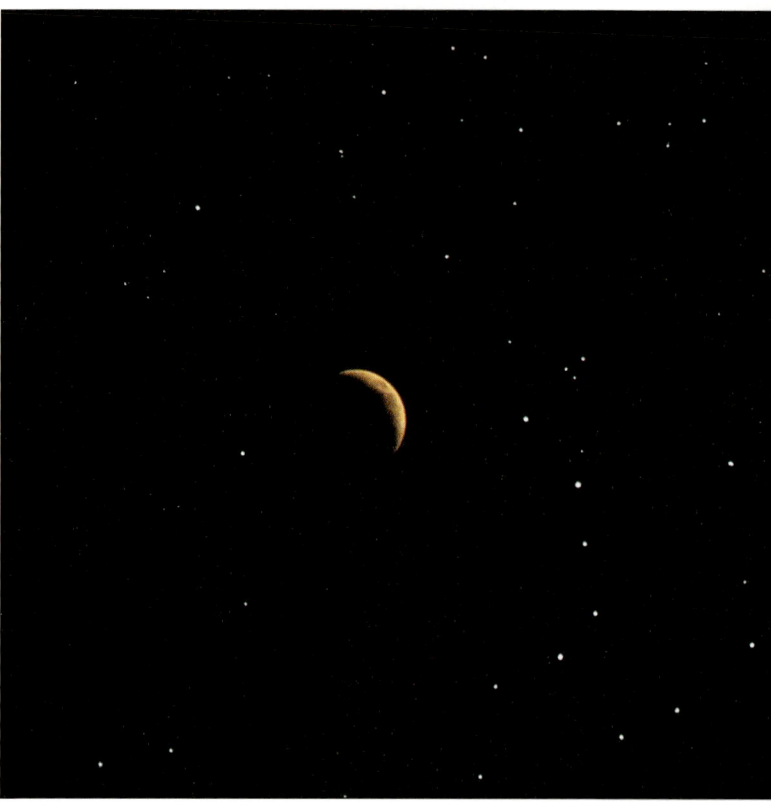

▲ The night sky does not stay constant. As the Earth turns the stars appear to rise in the east and set in the west. The star patterns also move depending on the time of year and your position on the surface of the Earth.

▲ Io is one of the four largest moons of the planet Jupiter. The moons were discovered by Galileo in 1610 using the first type of astronomical telescope. The moons were also discovered quite separately by Simon Marius (1570–1624), a German astronomer who gave them the names Io, Europa, Ganymede and Callisto.

On a clear night, away from the city lights, you can see a lot in the sky with just your own eyes – the moon, patterns of stars, and occasionally other planets. Once telescopes had been invented, star gazers could see a lot more and were soon making new discoveries. Galileo used one of the first telescopes to observe new moons, planets, sunspots and show that the Earth actually does move around the Sun.

In the year that Galileo died, 1642, another important scientist, Isaac Newton, was born. Newton was an English mathematician and physicist whose work changed the way people thought about the Earth and the movement of the planets.

▲ Newton's first reflecting telescope based on a design of 1668, is much the same as telescopes used by amateur astronomers today.

ISAAC NEWTON

Newton was an enormously influential scientist. He wrote a book called *Philosophiae Naturalis Principia Mathematica* in which he described mathematically his ideas about forces, motion and gravity and used them to explain the movement of the moon and the planets. His ideas have survived into the present century and for everyday purposes provide a good working explanation for the solar system. For other work, however, scientists would now use ideas put forward by German physicist, Albert Einstein (1879–1955), in the first part of the twentieth century.

Newton invented a reflecting telescope which used mirrors instead of lenses. This helped him to make fresh discoveries and first suggest the idea that the pull of gravity acts between any two objects in the universe and that gravity extends throughout space.

Gravity is universal. But we only notice it when the objects involved are really massive, like the Sun and the Earth, or the moon and the Earth. Without gravity, galaxies would not exist, the planets would not stay in orbit around the Sun, and our feet would not stay securely on the ground.

 # STAR PATTERNS AND GALAXIES

The Ancient Egyptians, the Greeks and North American Indians all spotted patterns in the stars and made up stories around them. Today, we have names like Taurus (the bull), Orion the Hunter, the Great Bear, Canis Minor (little dog) and Canis Major (big dog) but not many people today learn the stories associated with them.

If you look up into the sky on a clear night, you will see thousands of stars, especially if you are well away from street lights. The star patterns, or constellations, are difficult to see unless you have someone to point them out to you. The constellation of Orion, however, is very distinctive and can be seen from most parts of the world. In the northern hemisphere, the Plough is another pattern that is fairly easy to pick out. In the southern hemisphere, you can often see the Southern Cross.

◀ The Southern Cross is very easy to see in the night sky of the southern hemisphere. Four bright stars show the ends of the arms of the cross and a faint star in the middle shows where the arms meet.

◀ The Plough is sometimes called the Saucepan because of its shape. To find it, you need to look to the north. The two stars at the end of the pan point straight to the Pole Star, which always stays in the same position in the sky over the North Pole. The Plough changes position through the year so that sometimes the pan handle is pointing down and the pan itself is sideways.

◀ Orion the Hunter is easy to see because of the three stars that form the hunter's belt. From the northern hemisphere, it is best seen looking south on a clear night in January. From the southern hemisphere, it is visible in the northern sky for most of the year.

Above the three stars in the belt are two bright stars. The pinkish one on the left is called Betelgeuse and the one on the right is called Bellatrix. Below the belt is a fuzzy red glow that is known as the Great Nebula. The bright star on the bottom right is called Rigel.

In reality, stars exist in large collections or 'cities of stars' called galaxies. Some galaxies contain several million stars, others have thousands of millions. Our own galaxy is called the Milky Way. It is about 100,000 light-years across – that is the distance that light would travel in 100,000 years. Our galaxy belongs to what is called a 'local group' of about thirty galaxies. Another member of the group is the Andromeda Galaxy which can be seen in the night sky as a hazy distant patch, about 2.5 million light-years away.

Beyond our local group, there are many more very distant galaxies. The nearest is about 8 million light-years away – if you could see the light from the galaxy it would have left there 8 million years ago.

Galaxies come in different sizes and shapes. Some are spiral-shaped, some elliptical-shaped and some are irregular-shaped. Both the Milky Way and Andromeda are spiral galaxies.

▼ The Andromeda Galaxy is a giant spiral galaxy containing possibly 400,000 million stars. It has two much smaller companion galaxies: the bright object below it in the picture is an irregular galaxy; and the bright star-like object above the centre is an elliptical galaxy.

 # OUR STAR – THE SUN

Ancient peoples depended completely on the Sun for warmth and light, and it is not really surprising that they looked on the Sun as a god. The Greek, Roman and Egyptian civilizations all had a special god linked with the Sun. Even now, sunshine has an immense effect on our daily lives – and life certainly could not exist without it.

▲ This pottery sculpture is in the Museum of Popular Art in Mexico. It shows the head of the Mayan Sun god held in the jaws of the Earth monster. Sun worship by the Mayan civilization was at its peak in Mexico between the fourth and eighth centuries AD.

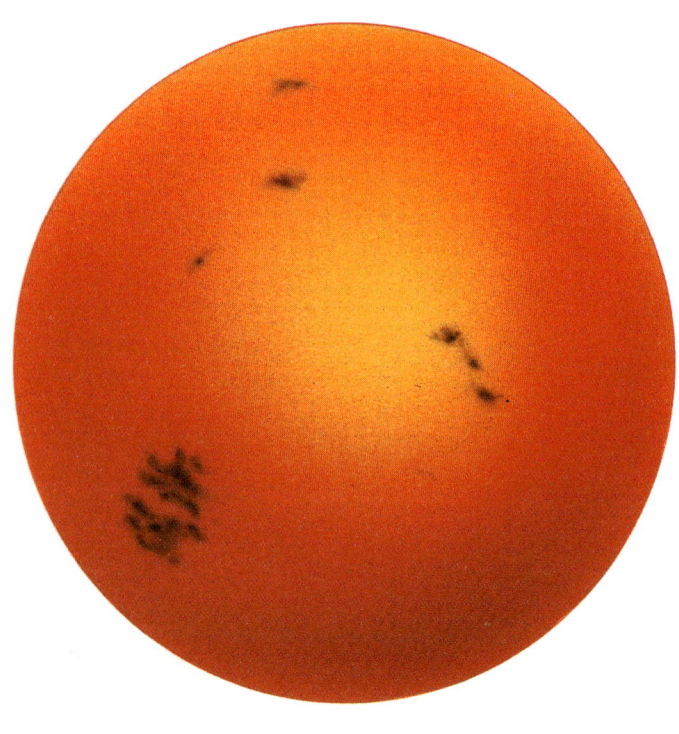

▲ The Sun is a seething mass of gas. Strong convection currents move hot gas from the inside to the surface. Sometimes strong local magnetic fields prevent this mixing from taking place causing a cooler patch on the surface. This is a sunspot.

After the invention of telescopes astronomers such as Galileo could see that the Sun was not a perfect, glowing ball but was speckled with black spots, which we call sunspots. Sunspots have diameters bigger than the Earth's diameter. They are places on the surface of the Sun where the temperature is 2,000°C lower than elsewhere on the surface. This causes the difference in colour. We also know now that the Sun spins around on its own axis once every 27 days, so sunspots appear to move. Astronomers began keeping records of sunspots in 1755. In May 1778, the sunspot count was 239. This record was not exceeded until October 1957, when the count was 263.

◀ The Sun's corona during the total solar eclipse that occurred on 11 July 1991 was visible from Hawaii, California and Mexico. The bright spot top left appears because the solar disc becomes visible through valleys on the moon. The eclipse lasted for six minutes and fifty-four seconds.

Sometimes the moon passes between the Sun and the Earth casting a shadow on to the planet. This is called a solar eclipse. A clay tablet unearthed in Syria contains the oldest known record of an eclipse, which happened on 5 March 1223 BC.

During an eclipse, astronomers are able to study the halo of gas that surrounds the Sun. It is called the corona and stretches for millions of kilometres out into space. Normally it is impossible to see the corona because of the brightness of the Sun, but it is visible during an eclipse. Massive plumes of hot gas can be seen shooting out into space at speeds up to 1,000 kilometres per second. (That is fast – about one three-hundredths of the speed of light.) The gas is hydrogen and the flares are known as prominences.

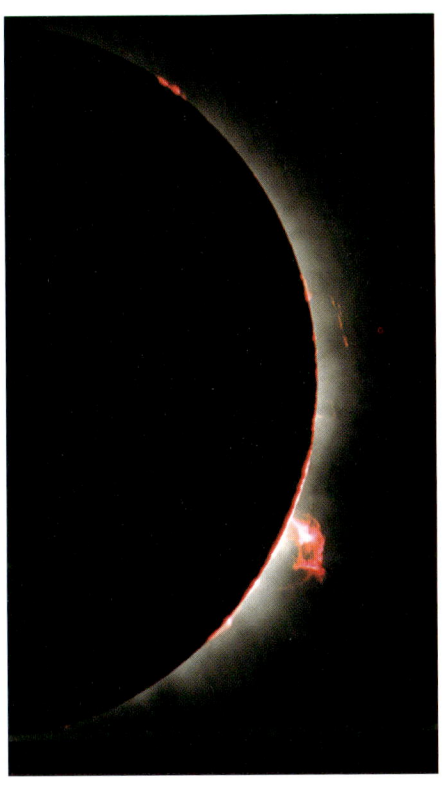

▲ The white halo at the edge of the eclipse is the solar corona. The temperature is very high – about 1 million degrees Celsius. The pink-coloured solar prominence extends thousands of kilometres into space.

 FORTHCOMING TOTAL ECLIPSES

Astronomers can work out very accurately when eclipses are going to occur. It may be that you will be able to see one of the eclipses due to happen between now and the year 2000.

Date	Where it will be visible
9 March 1997	Russia, Arctic
26 February 1998	Pacific, Central America
11 August 1999	Atlantic, Europe, UK, India

OUR MOON AND OTHERS

For our ancestors, the moon was the only source of light during the dark hours and moon worship was widespread. Greeks, Romans and Egyptians had gods or goddesses who were linked with the moon. Careful observation of the moon was important because it helped people to keep track of time and the seasons. Slowly the idea that the moon was a body moving round a spherical Earth became accepted.

When we look up into a clear night sky, the biggest object we see is the moon. This is, quite simply, because the moon is near to us compared to other objects in space. Until the middle of the twentieth century, its study was mostly the work of amateur astronomers.

Half moon

Full moon

Crescent moon

▲ Each month the moon seems to grow and then shrink again. When it grows we say it is waxing and when it shrinks we say it is waning. These changes are known as the phases of the moon.

We see the moon because sunlight falls on it and is reflected back towards us on Earth. The moon goes round the Earth every 28 days and we see it from many different angles. The different views we have of the moon are called phases, but we only ever see one side of the moon. The side of the moon that we do see is fascinating when viewed through a telescope or binoculars. The first people viewing it this way saw areas on the moon that they thought were seas or oceans, and they gave each 'sea' its own name. An Italian teacher called Giovanni Riccioli published a moon map in 1651 and his system of names is still in use today.

▼ This is the full moon as it was seen from Maryland, USA in 1982. The bright crater at the bottom is called Tycho.

 **OTHER MOONS**

The Earth is not the only planet with a moon. Most other planets in the solar system have moons orbiting round them. Some have several moons and ring systems, and scientists are unsure exactly how many moons there are.

Name of planet	Number of known moons
Mercury	0
Venus	0
Earth	1
Mars	2
Jupiter	16
Saturn	18
Uranus	15
Neptune	8
Pluto	1

▼ The planet Pluto and its moon Charon are so close together that eclipses of the sun are common as they orbit each other. This is an artist's impression of what they look like.

Pluto

Charon

We now know that these oceans or lakes are large craters on the moon's surface filled with lava that has solidified. The moon has no air, water, wind or indeed any weather of any kind. Because of this the surface remains the same and nothing ever changes except when objects from space hit the surface. Without an atmosphere, flying fragments can fall to the moon without burning up. Most fragments falling to Earth burn up in the atmosphere because the friction between the fragments and the air is so great they glow with heat. This is why the moon is covered with so many craters and the Earth has far fewer.

15

 # SATELLITES AROUND THE EARTH

The first artificial satellite to orbit the Earth was launched by a Russian rocket on 4 October 1957 and was called SPUTNIK I. It was about the size of a beach ball. SPUTNIK survived for ninety-two days before it fell out of orbit and burned up after re-entering the atmosphere.

Nowadays, a huge variety of satellites from many different countries orbit our planet. You can often see them in the night sky, looking like moving stars. Some are used to send telephone messages, radio and television programmes – these are called communications satellites. Others are used to explore the planet and to monitor what is happening on the Earth's surface.

 ## THE ELECTROMAGNETIC SPECTRUM

| gamma rays | X-rays | ultraviolet | visible light | infra-red | microwaves | UHF VHF | radio waves |

People see things with their eyes by collecting light waves which are visible to the human eye. Light waves are part of a whole family of waves known as the electromagnetic spectrum. Although we cannot see most of these waves, they can be used to send information and can be converted into pictures that we can see.

The existence of these invisible waves was noticed in 1895 when the German physicist, Wilhelm Conrad von Röntgen (1845–1923), detected invisible rays that he called X-rays. Today, satellites scan the Earth particularly in the infra-red, visible and ultraviolet parts of the spectrum. Different wavelengths provide different kinds of information. Invisible wavelengths can be converted by computer to give false-colour pictures.

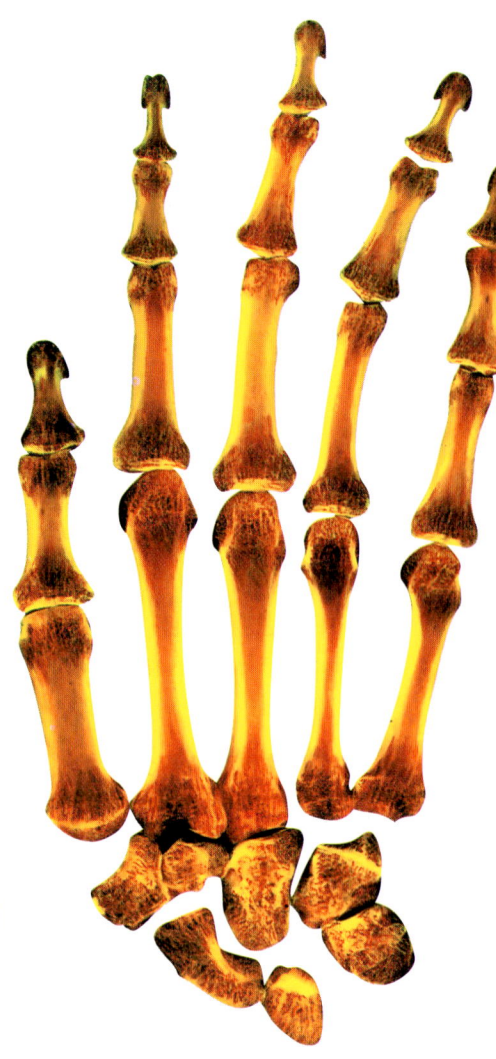

▲ This false colour X-ray picture shows the bones of the human hand. In 1896 Röntgen astonished the world with an X-ray picture of his wife's hand. It was the first time that people had seen the effects of radiation.

▲ The INTELSAT family of communication satellites were put into geostationary orbits above the Pacific Ocean during the early 1990s. Each satellite can handle 90,000 voice channels and three television channels at the same time. They are expected to have a lifetime of fifteen years. This is an artist's impression of INTELSAT 7.

▼ This false colour picture of North and South America is made up of several pictures taken by the NOAA satellites. The reddish-brown colour shows areas of lush vegetation such as the Amazon rainforest. You can also see the Rocky Mountains and the Andes running down the left sides of the continents.

Satellites orbiting the Earth take photographs which are then sent back to the ground using radio waves as a message carrier. The pictures may be used in searching for oil, studying the way crops grow, finding precious minerals, searching for pollution, weather forecasting or mapping the Earth's surface. Governments also use them to spy on other countries.

Some satellites stay in orbit over exactly the same place on Earth in what is called a geostationary orbit. To do this they have to be more than 35,000 kilometres above us and travel faster than the Earth so that they can keep pace with it.

ROCKETS, SHUTTLES, SPACE STATIONS

Firework rockets were made by the Chinese more than 1,000 years ago – the jet of hot gas required to propel the rocket skywards was produced by lighting gunpowder. Modern rockets work in a similar way. Space vehicles are launched by rockets powerful enough to escape the Earth's gravity.

By the middle of the twentieth century, the development of rocket fuels and computers had made the launching of spacecraft a real possiblity. The vast resources required for space exploration can only be provided by governments and the work achieved by teams of dedicated people. In 1958, the president of the USA set up the National Aeronautics and Space Administration (NASA) to manage the USA's space programme. The Soviet Union also gave the exploration of space a high priority. The two countries competed to be first in space and to put an astronaut on the moon.

In 1926, the American rocket scientist, Robert Goddard (1882–1945), launched the first successful rocket with an engine that burned liquid fuel. In the Second World War, the German rocket engineer, Wernher von Braun (1912–1977) made war rockets that were used to attack London in 1942. After the war, von Braun joined the US space team and in 1969, a giant American Saturn V rocket sent the first moon landing craft on its way.

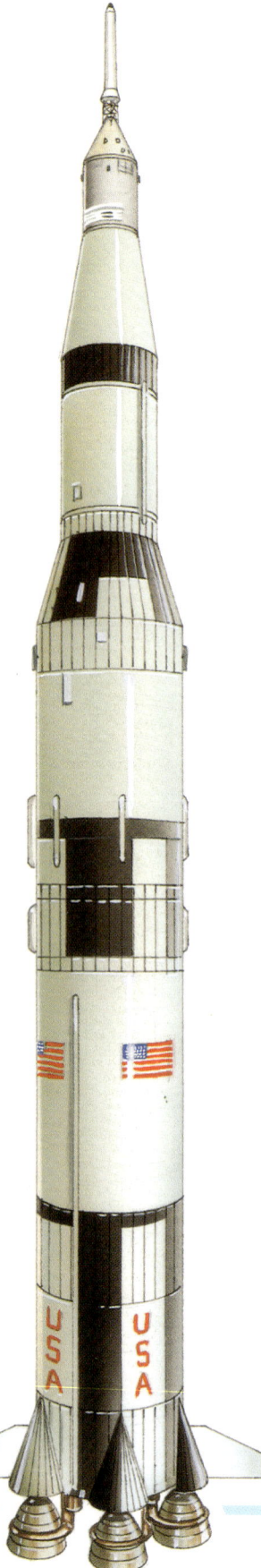

◀ Saturn V.

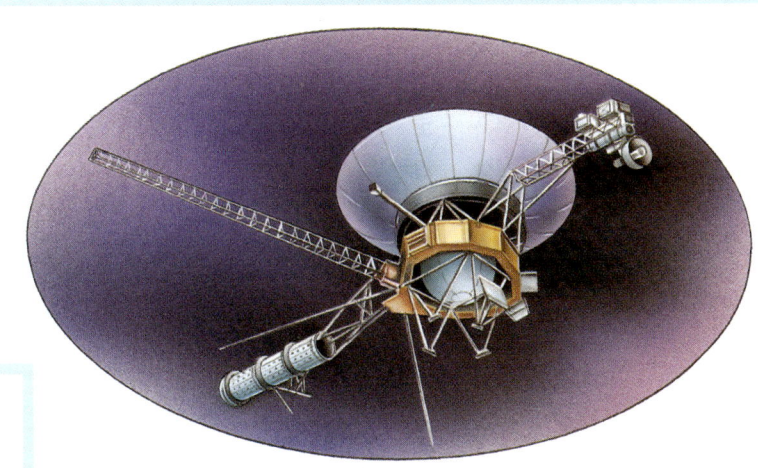

SPACE TRAVEL

One of the main limits to space travel is the speed at which we can move. One of the faster space probes was Voyager 2, launched in 1977 from the Kennedy Space Centre. Voyager took four years to reach Saturn, another five years to reach Uranus (in 1986) and arrived at Neptune by 1989, eleven years after its launch. Voyager space probes travel at about 20 kilometres per second. Now imagine travelling at this speed to the nearest star, over 40 million million kilometres away. At Voyager speed this would take just over 60,000 years.

Russian scientists concentrated on building a space station in permanent orbit above the Earth and sending teams of astronauts up there from time to time to carry out experiments. The Mir space station was launched in 1986 and has been operating successfully ever since.

▼ A space shuttle gliding in to land.

Most space vehicles are launched into space and never return. But in 1981, *Columbia*, the first reusable space shuttle was launched. The space shuttle fleet is the backbone of the US space programme. A shuttle takes off like a rocket and returns to Earth as a glider. On its way up it sheds its external fuel tank and its twin extra rocket boosters. Once in orbit 250 kilometres above the Earth, its massive bay doors open, allowing it to place a satellite into Earth orbit. When returning to Earth it uses its rocket engines to come out of orbit, re-enters the atmosphere and eventually glides down on to a runway like a plane.

TRAVEL TO THE MOON AND BACK

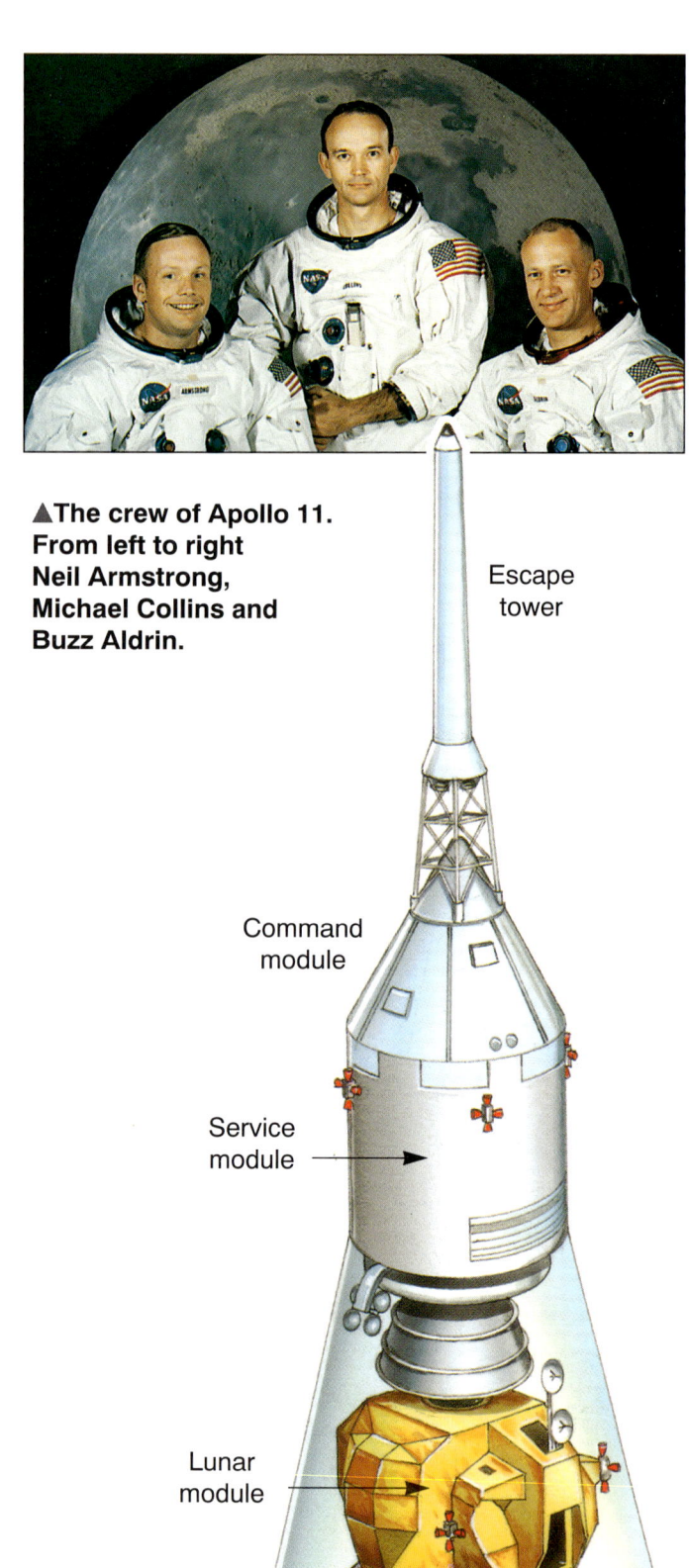

▲ The crew of Apollo 11. From left to right Neil Armstrong, Michael Collins and Buzz Aldrin.

Escape tower

Command module

Service module

Lunar module

The Apollo programme was the name given to the United States space programme which began in 1961. Its aim was to land astronauts on the moon before 1970. There were ten experimental flights followed by seven moon landings.

The first landing on the moon was in 1969 – three American astronauts: Neil Armstrong, Buzz Aldrin and Michael Collins were launched on an epic mission on 16 July. The huge Saturn V rocket took off with a two-part spacecraft fitting snugly inside its nose.

To provide enough power to escape the Earth's gravity the rocket had three separate stages. Each stage burned and separated in turn. After the final burn, Apollo 11 was heading for the moon.

Michael Collins stayed with the command module on 21 July, orbiting the moon while Armstrong and Aldrin dropped down to the moon's surface in Eagle, the lunar module. As Armstrong stepped forth his famous words crackled back to Earth, *'That's one small step for man, one giant leap for mankind.'*

Millions of people watched and listened on television as first Armstrong and then Aldrin took their first steps on the moon.

◀ The moon astronauts travelled inside the command module in the nose cone of the Saturn V rocket. Also in the nose cone was a service module full of equipment and the lunar module.

Imagine the sensation of being on the moon. The moon has no atmosphere, so there is no wind or rain and no sound because it has no air in which to travel. The footprints left by the first two astronauts are still there, in the moon dust, more than twenty-five years later because there is nothing to blow or wash the steps away. The moon's gravity is six times weaker than the Earth's; it is a much smaller object. The weight of each astronaut was six times smaller than their weight on Earth. If Armstrong had been a high-jumper he probably could have jumped about thirty feet on the moon.

▲ Moon astronauts carried out experiments and collected samples of rock and soil which they brought back to Earth.

☀ SURFACE TEMPERATURE

The moon has no atmosphere and no clouds, so the temperature there by day is a boiling hot 117°C. By night, without the clouds to retain the heat, it cools to a freezing −162°C. This is much chillier than even the coldest Siberian winter.

To cope with the tremendous heat and cold, the astronauts wore special space suits. These protected them from the fierceness of the Sun's rays, insulated them from the intense cold at night and provided them with oxygen to breathe.

▶ It takes nearly two and half hours for an astronaut to put on a space suit. First there is special underwear that keeps the astronaut cool. Then the trousers are put on followed by the top and the gloves. Last of all the helmet is fitted into place. The pack on the back provides cooling water, oxygen and voice communication.

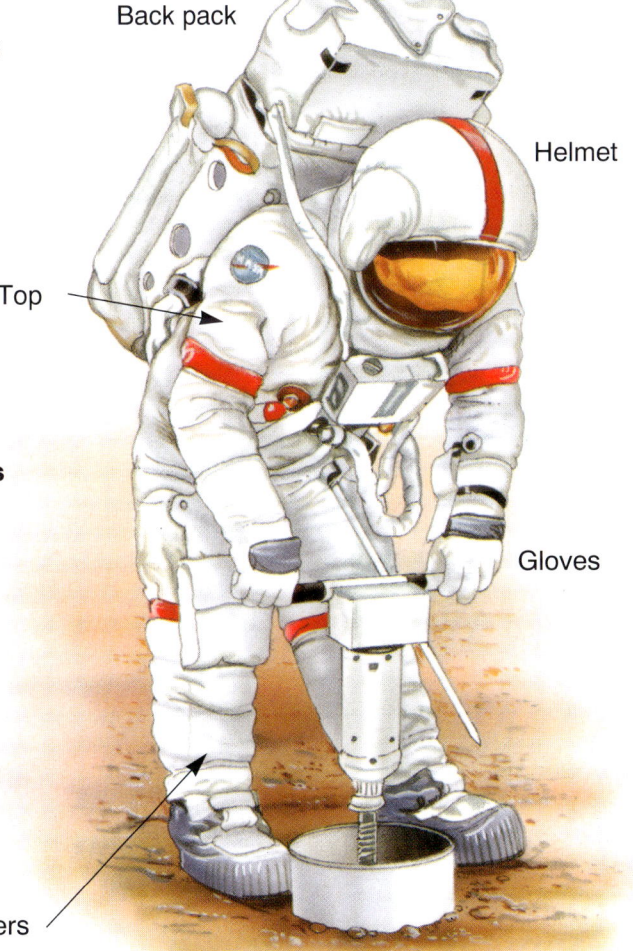

21

THE INNER PLANETS

Our Earth is just one of the nine planets that orbit the Sun. Each planet has its own unique environment. Most have moons, some do not. Some are very hot; the ones further from the Sun are much colder. Each takes a different time to complete one orbit of the Sun – a time that varies between eighty-eight days for the nearest to 248 years for the furthest. The planets nearest the Sun are called the inner planets: Mercury, Venus, Earth, and Mars. These are the ones we know most about because they are quite near to Earth.

▲ The view of Mercury as Mariner 10 approached it for the first time on 29 March 1974. Hundreds of craters have been formed by flying rocks bombarding the planet.

◀ The Magellan space probe was despatched to Venus in May 1989. Its purpose was to map the surface of Venus using a radar system that would penetrate the dense clouds of poisonous gas. In October 1994, the probe was allowed to make a controlled fall into the Venusian atmosphere, collecting data until it finally burned up. This is an artist's impression of how it might have looked.

Venus is the planet we can see most often in the night sky, and sometimes even by day. People once thought that this planet was a beautiful place with rich, lush plant life. We now know that it is more like a vision of hell. Both the Russians and the Americans have sent probes to Venus.

Venus has clouds of acid and a thick, dense atmosphere of carbon dioxide which traps in the Sun's heat with a terrific greenhouse effect – its temperature reaches 475°C. The pressure of Venus' atmosphere is about twenty times our own atmospheric pressure – an astronaut landing on Venus would be simultaneously roasted to death and suffocated.

Mercury was first seen through a telescope by Johannes Hevelius in the fifteenth century. It is a small lump of rock, only half as big again as our moon. There are no clouds to protect it from the Sun or to keep the heat in at night, so during the day its temperature is 420°C, and at night it falls to −180°C. Astronomers had a close look at Mercury in 1974 with the space probe Mariner 10.

▼ A view of the Martian landscape sent back to Earth by Viking 1 in 1976. The atmosphere is carbon dioxide, there are frozen carbon dioxide caps at the poles, and weather patterns, but no life.

Mars is a planet that has captured the imagination of many people. Some once thought that there were canals and vegetation on Mars and that there might be intelligent life on the planet – the Martians. Viking space probes landed on Mars from the USA in 1976 proving absolutely that there is no life there. Iron-rich minerals in the surface rocks cause the red colour of the planet.

 ## FACTS ABOUT THE INNER PLANETS

Name	Approximate size compared with Earth	Distance from the sun (millions of kilometres)	Temperature on the surface (°C)	Time to orbit the sun	Number of moons
Mercury	one-third	58	350	88 days	0
Venus	two-thirds	108	480	225 days	0
Earth	—	150	22	365 days	1
Mars	half	228	−23	2 years	2

THE OUTER PLANETS

There are five planets beyond Mars in our solar system – four of them are really big planets and are actually made of gases. Most of our knowledge about the outer planets comes from four American space probes: Pioneer 10, Pioneer 11, Voyager 1 and Voyager 2. The last of these visited Jupiter, Saturn, Uranus and Neptune in turn between 1979 and 1989.

◀ Jupiter is the largest of all the planets. If we could put all the other planets together and squash them inside Jupiter, we would fill less than half its volume. The red spot on Jupiter is a giant storm stretching more than 30,000 kilometres across and rising eight kilometres above the surrounding clouds. The red colour may be caused by phosphorus. A ring system was discovered around Jupiter in 1979.

FACTS ABOUT THE OUTER PLANETS

Name	Approximate size compared with Earth	Distance from the sun (millions of kilometres)	Temperature on the surface (°C)	Time to orbit the sun	Number of moons
Jupiter	11 times	778	−110	12 years	16
Saturn	9 times	1,425	−180	29 years	18
Uranus	4 times	2,867	−210	84 years	15
Neptune	nearly 4 times	4,497	−220	165 years	8
Pluto	one-third	5,900	−230	248 years	1

Perhaps the most beautiful planet is Saturn, with its lovely rings that were first discovered by the Dutch physicist, Christian Huygens (1629–1693) in 1656. Saturn spins at a terrific rate, once every 10.5 hours, so its gases bulge at the Equator giving it a slightly squashed appearance. The Voyager 2 probes discovered nine previously unknown moons.

▶ Uranus is tipped on its side. At present the North Pole is pointing towards the Sun and will stay in daylight until 2007. Afterwards there will be forty-two years of darkness while the South Pole points towards the Sun.

▲ Voyager 2 showed that Saturn's rings are made up of ice and rock circling endlessly around the planet.

▲ Neptune has a great dark spot which is a hugh whirlwind the size of the Earth. Voyager 2 measured winds up to 325 metres per second.

▼ Little Pluto may be visited by a space probe in the next century.

The further out the planets are in the solar system, the less we know about them. The outer three are Uranus, Neptune and Pluto. Uranus is the largest and was discovered in 1781 by the German-born astronomer William Herschel (1738–1822). We now know that it has fifteen moons and eleven dark rings which possibly contain a lot of carbon.

Neptune was discovered in 1846. The French scientist, Urbain Le Verrier, and the British scientist, John Couch Adams were studying Uranus separately and both noticed it was behaving in a strange way. They decided this was because of the gravity of another planet. They sent their calculations to the observatory in Berlin where German astronomers, Johann Galle and Heinrich d'Arrest, used them to locate the new planet.

The most distant planet, Pluto, was discovered by American astronomer, Clyde Tombaugh (1906–), in 1930 and its moon, Charon, by the American astronomer James Christy, working at the US Naval Observatory in 1978. Pluto can only be seen through a giant telescope and has never been visited by a space probe. It is small, bitterly cold and has an unusual orbit which sometimes takes it inside the orbit of Neptune.

COMETS AND SHOOTING STARS

From looking at diagrams of the solar system with planets neatly orbiting the Sun, you might imagine that space is a clean, tidy, well-ordered place. Nothing could be further from the truth. Our solar system is littered with flying rocks, dust and ice particles which are constantly colliding with the planets and their moons. Some people believe that the extinction of the dinosaurs was caused by a giant comet banging into the Earth millions of years ago. More recently, in July 1994, a large comet collided with Jupiter and astronomers were able to study the effects from telescopes on Earth.

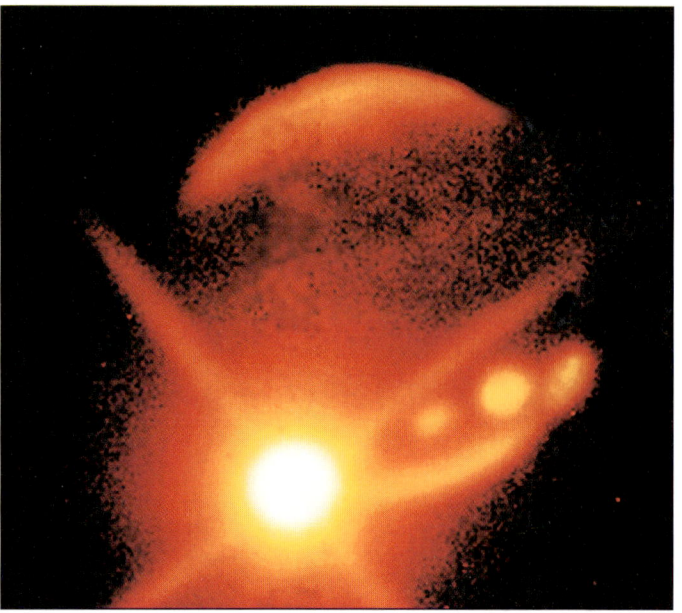
▲ When Comet Shoemaker-Levy 9 hit Jupiter in July 1994, it broke up into more than twenty pieces. This picture, taken by the Mount Stromlo Observatory in Australia, shows the fireball (20,000 km in diameter) created by one piece that hit the planet at 10.18 GMT on 18 July.

▼ Comet Halley's most recent visit, photographed here from Australia, was in 1986. Several space probes were launched or diverted to observe Halley. These missions confirmed many of the ideas astronomers had about comets.

Comets are rather like large dirty snowballs – lumps of rock and ice that travel around the Sun in strangely shaped orbits. This is why they may collide with planets, when the orbits cross. The best known comet is Halley's comet which we can see from Earth every seventy-six years. Edmond Halley was a British astronomer born in 1656 who suggested that since the comets sighted in 1531, 1607 and 1682 had identical orbits, they could be the same comet. He predicted that the comet would reappear in 1758. Halley died in 1742, so he did not live to see the comet return – but his suggestion proved to be correct. If you live until the year 2062 you will see Comet Halley for yourself.

▶ This 7.5 kg rock was discovered by US scientists in the Elephant Moraine region of Antarctica. It is a meteorite which may have resulted from the impact of a much larger meteorite on Mars. The rock is 1,300 million years old.

 ASTEROIDS

As well as comets, there are pieces of rock called asteroids orbiting around the Sun. They are most common in the band between Jupiter and Mars known as the asteroid belt. Some asteroids are nearly as big as small planets and it is difficult to define the difference between them. Asteroids are the leftovers from the time when the solar system was formed.

The Earth is frequently bombarded with small pieces of rock that burn up in the atmosphere. These burning rocks are called shooting stars, or meteors, and they can sometimes be seen in the sky on a clear night. The best time to look out for shooting stars is when the Earth's orbit takes us through the path of a comet's tail. The atmosphere is very good at protecting the Earth from flying debris. This is why Earth has far fewer craters than the moon. Occasionally a bigger rock does last long enough to reach the ground and we call it a meteorite. When large meteorites do crash to Earth they have dramatic effects.

▶ Barringer Crater in northern Arizona, USA, was formed by a meteorite impact about 25,000 years ago. It is 200 metres deep and about 800 metres across.

SPACE TRAVEL – UP AND DOWN

In May 1991, the Juno mission involved the British astronaut Helen Sharman in a visit to the Russian Mir space station. The rocket that took the astronauts into orbit had three stages. The first stage had four engines and the second and third just one each. At take off, the engines gradually built up their thrust (pushing force) until it was larger than the combined weight of the rocket and the Soyuz craft. When the thrust exceeded the total weight, lift-off began.

Once in orbit the Soyuz craft was to connect with the Mir space station. This was not an easy task. On the Juno mission, the manoeuvre happened two days after the launch and took six burns of the engine to get the craft into position. They docked with a bump, a bit like a ship mooring at harbour.

▲ Alexei Leonov (far right), director of training at Moscow's Star City and the first human being to walk in space in March 1965, is seen here in 1991 talking to a new generation. Britain's first astronaut, Helen Sharman, Sergei Kirkalev (left) and Anatoli Artsebarski (right) are about to depart for the Baikonur Cosmodrome in Kazakhstan.

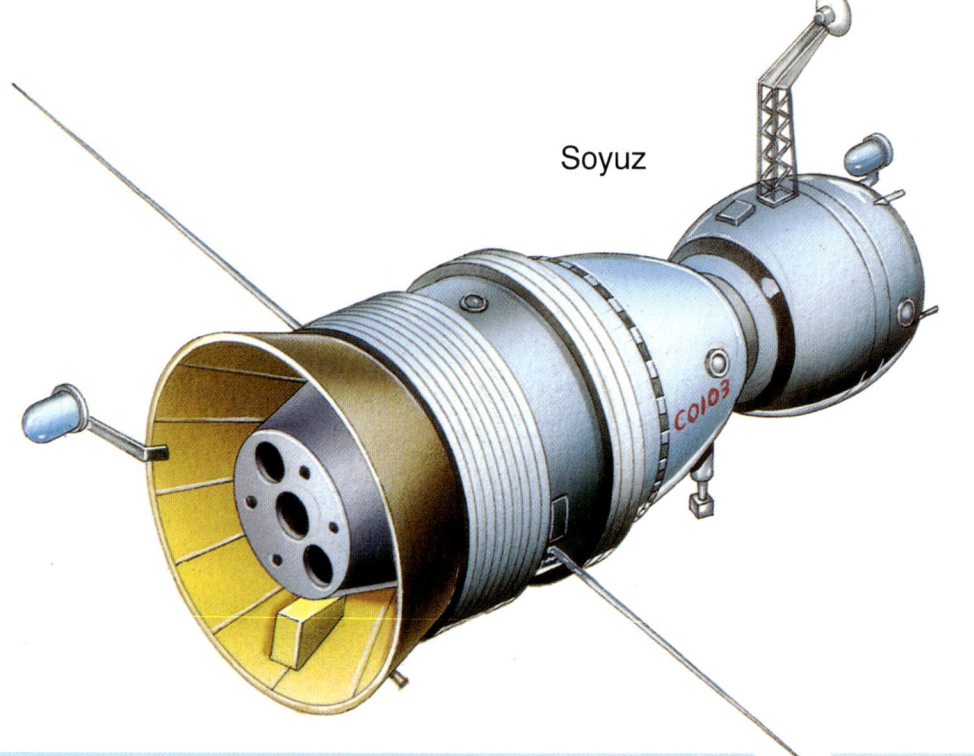

▲ A Soyuz crew ferry vehicle approaches the Mir space station. Small burns of the Soyuz engines put it in the correct position to connect to the Mir docking bay.

After docking, Helen Sharman joined Viktor Afanasyef and Musa Manarov, the Russian astronauts already on board Mir who had been living in space for over six months since 2 December 1990.

Living on Mir is like living on board a small train. Mir orbits the Earth sixteen times a day. That is about one and a half hours for each orbit. The astronauts experience sixteen dark times and sixteen light times in their day and they travel at a speed of 8 kilometres per second.

g-FORCES

About twelve seconds after the rocket lifts off, the astronauts begin to feel the force of gravity. It builds up to 3g – that means they feel three times as heavy as they do on Earth. Eventually after all the engines have been ignited and burned, there is a sudden drop to weightlessness. This is an experience like falling – in fact the spacecraft is falling into orbit. There is still gravity, but it is weaker. If there was no gravity at all, the craft would fly off into space. When the craft begins its descent, the g-forces build up again. This time they will feel a force 4.5 times the force of gravity at the surface of the Earth.

Mir

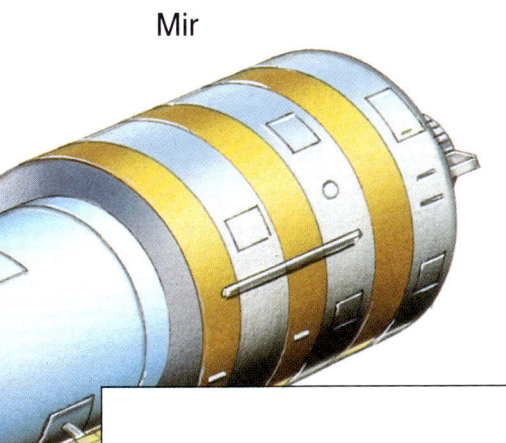

▼ Once the Soyuz descent module has landed in the Kazakhstan desert, the astronauts are collected by the ground crew.

Eight days later, Helen Sharman was due to make her descent although Sergei Kirkalev, her companion on the upward journey, was to be in orbit for ten months. The Soyuz craft disconnected from Mir and then the engines were fired at the exact moment to take it out of orbit in the right place over the Earth's surface. They wanted to land in a desert near Russia, not a freezing cold ocean.

High in the air the parachute opened and the Soyuz slowed down. Just before landing the the retro-rockets fired to soften the impact. The craft hit the Earth in the Kazakhstan desert and sent up a cloud of dust. Soyuz and its passengers bounced around and rolled over to one side.

When a spacecraft re-enters the Earth's atmosphere, friction with the air heats up the outside. A kind of a plasma forms and the capsule surface starts to melt. The craft is black and charred on arrival.

# ADAPTING TO LIFE IN SPACE

The first astronaut was the Russian, Yuri Gagarin, who made a flight lasting 1 hour 48 minutes in the shuttle Vostok 1, on 12 April 1961. Since then hundreds of astronauts from more than twenty countries have spent thousands of days in space. With each successive flight scientists learn more about the universe and the reactions of the human body to life in space.

▲ This pack of survival rations was carried by Yuri Gagarin on the world's first space flight. The pack with the red, yellow and blue label contains a protein mixture. There are rolls of 'pep-pills' and a chocolate bar wrapped in aluminium foil. Russian scientists were worried that it might take some time to find Gagarin when he returned to Earth and they supplied him with a survival kit.

As we travel towards space the Earth's atmosphere becomes thinner and its pressure becomes lower. This can have harmful effects on an astronaut's bodily functions.

The main product from breathing is carbon dioxide. On Earth when we breathe out the carbon dioxide is dispersed by a combination of wind and convection. In a space station there is no natural convection because hot air does not rise in a weightless situation. To prevent astronauts suffocating in their own exhaled breath, the air is circulated by fans. Long, flexible tubes are used to direct the air to different parts of the cabin. The air is kept fresh by removing the carbon dioxide and putting in more oxygen.

Human beings have been used to gravity throughout the millions of years of their evolution on Earth. Without it, even for short periods, strange things can happen. Body fluids and water rush to the heart, lungs and face. The bones lose minerals. The kidneys produce more urine. This upsets the salt balance of the body preventing muscles working properly. Astronauts need to do regular and often vigorous exercise to keep in shape.

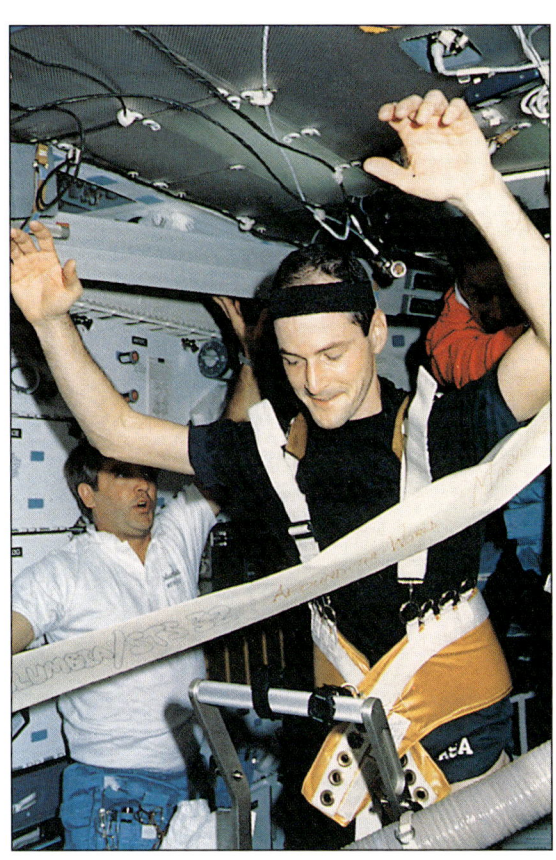

▶ American astronaut David Low runs a marathon on the treadmill exercise machine on board Shuttle *Columbia* in January 1990.

▼ High above the Earth, American astronaut Mark Lee tests out SAFER, a new EVA Rescue system, in September 1994.

Often astronauts need to carry out tasks outside the spacecraft. This is called extravehicular activity (EVA). EVA space suits need to be flexible and provide an atmosphere suitable for astronauts to function effectively. They are constructed from pressure-resistant materials, have several layers of insulation and an inner layer designed to transport water for cooling. A backpack provides the astronaut with an atmosphere of pure oxygen at a pressure less than half of that found on Earth. But the astronaut can only breathe in this sort of atmosphere for a few hours.

KEEPING CLEAN AND HEALTHY

Astronauts like to keep clean, especially with five of them living in a total space of 90 cubic metres (about the same as a room 6 metres by 5 metres by 3 metres). There is no running water so they have to wipe themselves down with special pre-packaged towels (like giant baby-wipes) and then dry off with another towel.

Cleaning their teeth is not easy – they cannot just take a gulp of water and spit it out again. Where would it go? They have to use the toothpaste and then swallow it – it does taste nice though.

Sleeping is also an important part of keeping healthy on a space mission. Loss of sleep can be caused by the excitement of being in space, noisy equipment (for example, the fans that circulate air round the cabin), communication systems, uncomfortable living conditions and staggered sleeping times. Every effort is made to cut down on noise when members of the crew are sleeping, but this is not always possible. It helps to wear ear plugs! It also helps to get inside a sleeping bag, which is tied to the spacecraft to stop the sleeper from floating around inside it.

▶ Commander John Young shaves during the first space shuttle mission in April 1981. There is a food tray below the mirror with different foods attached. Crew facilities are under constant development by NASA and each shuttle mission tests out new equipment.

A form of travel sickness which affects astronauts is known as space sickness. When travelling to space astronauts suffer from the effects of weightlessness – they feel as though they are continually falling. The sickness disappears after the brain has got used to its new environment, but even so, meeting, working or living with people who appear to be upside down can still give an astronaut space sickness. This is because messages received by the brain from the ear and the eye may often be in conflict.

▲ A whole-body zero-gravity shower is tested by NASA crew members for future use on a US space station. The equipment was tested in weightless conditions on board a jet aircraft. The aircraft flies a roller-coaster path which produces thirty-second periods of zero gravity. The astronauts call the jet the 'vomit comet'.

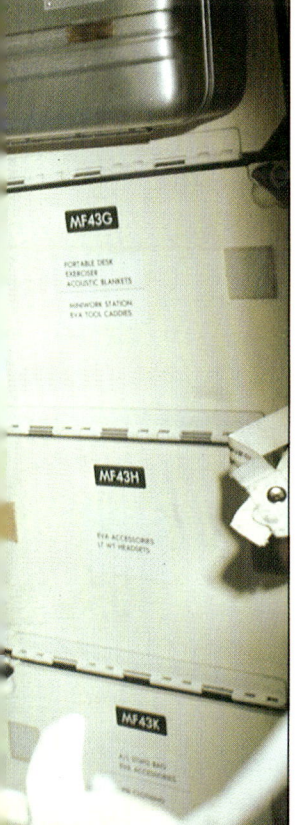

One of the main problems that astronauts face is living for long periods of time with the same companions in a confined environment. Space-station crews are carefully chosen for this reason. They must be able to work well together, be level-headed and have good common sense. These skills and others are important if people are to work effectively as a team. In a small spacecraft, it is impossible to go for a walk outside if someone is irritating you.

 EATING AND DRINKING

Astronauts eat things like: dried meat, dried fruit, dried potato or dried cabbage soup. In fact, most of their food is dried because it is lighter. They also have biscuits, nuts and cocoa. Fruit juice (blackcurrant and orange) comes in tubes so that they can squeeze it into the mouth – the fruit contains very important roughage. Space food must contain all the right ingredients for a balanced diet: protein, vitamins, fats and carbohydrates as well as minerals.

INPUTS AND OUTPUTS

The daily requirements for one astronaut are:

2.5 kg of water
0.9 kg of oxygen
0.7 kg of dried food

(notice that the dried food has the least mass, the water needed has the most)

The daily outputs are:

2.5 kg of urine
0.8 kg of carbon dioxide
0.2 kg of faeces

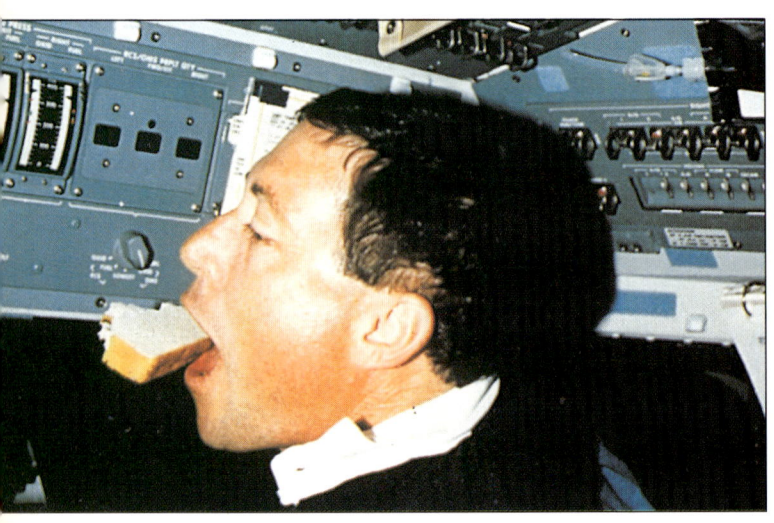

▲ American astronaut Michael Baker chases a sandwich during a shuttle flight in August 1991. Space meals have changed considerably since the early space flights when all food was like baby food.

Swallowing is not a problem in space because the tube connecting the mouth to the stomach is very muscular. The food is helped down the tube by slimy, slippery mucous – without this, swallowing could be a painful business. Nor is digestion a problem once the food has reached the stomach. Actually getting the food into the mouth, however, is a different matter. Sudden moves can cause it to float off the spoon. Spoons and other cutlery are usually smaller than normal utensils because too much food clinging to the top and bottom could make eating messy. Gravy, sauces and soups can cling to the sides of containers. Washing up is not an easy task inside a spacecraft.

Drinking is a problem. You cannot just pour water into your mouth if it has no weight. The force to get it into the mouth must come from somewhere. Some drinks can be sucked in with a straw. Others can be squeezed out of a tube. If they travel through the air to the astronaut's mouth they will form perfectly spherical balls of liquid, unlike the pear-shaped drops formed on Earth.

▼ At the Johnson Space Centre in the USA, scientists are testing a mock-up of a permanently manned space station under development by NASA. Astronauts will be expected to spend much longer in space once the space station is in position. This space toilet has been carefully designed to be unisex, pleasant and hygienic.

▲ Coffee is held in a special container on board the ninth space shuttle flight in November 1983.

Astronauts also need to go to the toilet. In weightless conditions this can be difficult – waste products, solid and liquid, would just float around if they had an ordinary toilet. A special toilet is needed which uses a fan to suck the waste into a special container. Some of the waste is recycled to make water and then oxygen – the rest is dried and sent into space.

35

THE EARTH IN SPACE

◀ The Earth is a beautiful sight from space, with the clouds and the oceans showing clearly.

▲ Human activities appear to be causing unwelcome and possibly permanent changes on the Earth like the acid rain pollution in European forests shown above. Satellites help us to measure variations in the global environment.

People once believed that the Earth was flat, and apparently some people still do – but once astronauts had been into orbit and taken pictures of our globe from space, they proved beyond doubt that we all live on a sphere. We know that the Earth spins around on its own axis once every twenty-four hours giving us day and night, and that it makes one complete orbit of the Sun each year giving us the seasons. We also know that the oceans are attracted by the gravity of the moon and the Sun causing high and low tides.

The English scientist, James Lovelock, suggested that Planet Earth is like a living thing which we must take care of and treat with respect. Everything we do to one part of the planet can affect the rest, just as cutting off a branch affects the whole tree. This idea is named the Gaia hypothesis after Gaia, the Greek goddess of life.

Modern astronomers still use telescopes to scan the skies but nowadays they are likely to be housed in large observatories, often found high on mountains with clear unpolluted skies. They will be controlled by computers which will also record and process the information collected by the telescopes. Even more useful are the telescopes that have been sent out into space, high above the Earth's surface where there is no interference from the atmosphere.

Astronomers also use new ways of seeing and observing. They use those electromagnetic waves that are invisible to human eyes to provide electronic computer images of distant bodies. Many modern telescopes have huge dishes that collect radio waves. Pulsars, discovered in 1968 by Jocelyn Bell working in Britain, are stars that give out hardly any light but emit very regular pulses of radio waves.

▼ The dish of a radio telescope at Pulkovo Observatory sited at an altitude of 2,070 metres near St Petersburg in Russia. The observatory is one of the oldest in the world. In the eighteenth century the first astronomical observations here were of the Sun. Today, research is concerned with radio astronomy, solar and stellar physics and questions in fundamental astronomy.

◀ The Hubble telescope produces clear, sharp optical pictures of objects in space. These are transmitted down to special receivers on Earth. The telescope is seen here moments after its release from Shuttle *Discovery* on 25 April 1990.

As well as looking outwards, we also look downwards on our planet. Satellites keep a watchful eye on our environment. They collect information about happenings such as rising temperatures, plagues of locusts, oil slicks and desertification.

In May 1995, a satellite called SEASTAR was launched to look for shoals of fish. This new 'fisherman's friend' can see shadows and colours in the ocean which indicate that a shoal of fish is around. Information from SEASTAR is transmitted to Earth and can be received by fishing boats with the correct identity code.

IS THERE LIFE OUT THERE?

One of the questions that people have been asking for centuries is: does life exist on another planet? Humans have weird and wonderful ideas about how life from another planet might look. Many science fiction films have been made picturing life arriving on Earth.

But what are the chances of life elsewhere? Hundreds of people have reported sightings of strange spacecraft in the sky in recent years – so many that perhaps they deserve to be taken seriously. Some of the photos of these unidentified flying objects (UFOs) look as if they could be real, although most have turned out to be fakes.

The place where most people have imagined there could be life is the planet Mars. Nowadays, Mars is bitterly cold and its poles are covered by ice caps of carbon dioxide. But there may once have been conditions to support life on Mars.

▲ The planet Mars was once thought to be home to other life forms – we now know it is quite dead.

◀ A copy of the plaque fixed to the side of Voyager 2, which is a message to other intelligent life forms in the universe.

We have two possible ways of finding other life in space: sending out spacecraft to search for it . . . or looking and listening for signals with our modern radio, light and X-ray telescopes. Messages were sent into space from a radio telescope in Puerto Rico in 1974 telling other possible life forms about our bodies, our Earth and our solar system. As far as we know, no message has come back yet, but remember that some stars (which might have their own solar systems) are so far away that a reply would take thousands of years to get back to us. Apparently, people started sending out messages into space to search for other intelligent beings in 1920 – those messages were only 75 light-years away in 1995 – a small distance compared with the size of the universe.

▲ Life on Earth is infinitely varied. It seems hard to believe that intelligent beings do not exist elsewhere in the universe.

A MESSAGE TO OTHER LIFE FORMS

Just in case a living being elsewhere in the universe ever encounters Voyager 2, Scientists fixed a plaque on to the side of the space probe showing a man, woman and child, and a simple map giving our position in space.

They also attached a record containing music and greetings in many different languages, and over 100 pictures including a human skeleton, a mountain, an ocean, and a picture of Earth from space.

What are the chances of life in another solar system? Some scientists have calculated that the chances are high. They argue that there are so many billions of stars in the universe that the chances of one having a solar system like the Sun's are quite good. The chances of that solar system having a planet which could support life are also reasonable. Therefore there may be a planet orbiting in a solar system like ours with life on it, which may just have evolved into intelligent life. Who knows? We cannot rule it out on scientific grounds, even if the mathematical chances are quite small. What do you think? Is there intelligent life somewhere out there? Next time you gaze at the night sky, ponder on it.

# THE LIFE AND DEATH OF STARS

▼ The supernova (bottom right) discovered on 23 February 1987 near to the Tarantula nebula (left).

Stars are giant balls of glowing gas which give out infra-red (heat), light and other waves. Some stars are as much as twenty times bigger than our Sun. Astronomers have discovered that many of these large stars are blue-white in colour because they are so hot. These rare stars are called blue giants. Others are only one tenth of the size of the Sun and are a reddish colour because they are cooler. These are known as red dwarfs. The life cycle of a star depends on its size – the biggest stars often last for only millions of years because they use their hydrogen gas up quickly. Smaller stars, like our Sun, last for thousands of millions of years.

Each star begins from a nebula: a large cloud of dust and gas. A star is formed when the gas shrinks under the pull of gravity to occupy a much smaller volume. As the nebula shrinks the gas heats up. Eventually nuclear reactions begin in which hydrogen atoms are fused together releasing enormous energy, and a star is born. As long as there is plenty of hydrogen to keep the nuclear reactions going, the star shines brightly. But near the end of its life, the hydrogen starts to run out and the star may swell up to become a red giant.

Many stars then shrink to become white dwarfs. But some large stars explode in a supernova, a massive star explosion.

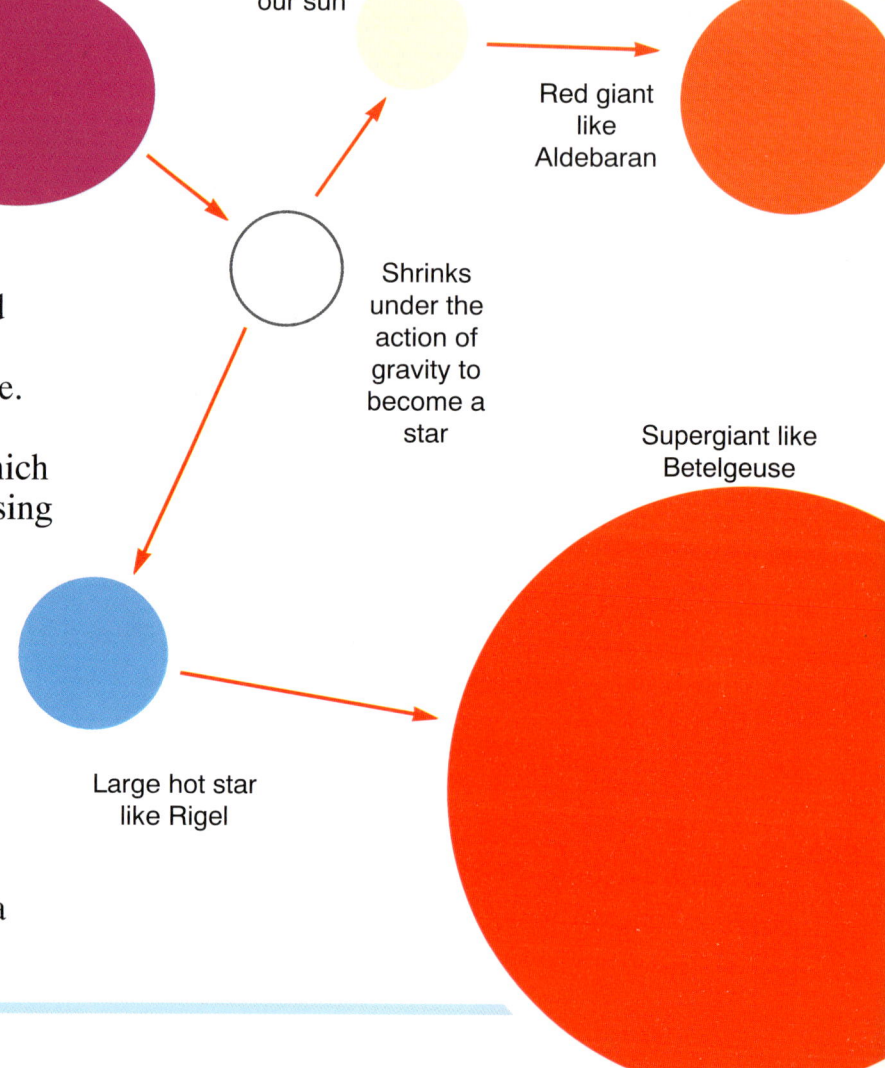

A supernova was first recorded in China in 1006. A supernova is very bright in the sky for a time before it eventually fades. Sometimes a pulsar is left in its place, sending out pulses of radio waves. But some scientists believe that occasionally a black hole is formed from a dying star. A black hole has such a strong gravitational pull that nothing, not even light can escape. However, we think they may send out signals as X-rays.

HOTTER AND COOLER STARS

Type	Colour	
O	blue	**hottest**
B	blue-white	
A	white	
F	yellow-white	
G	yellow	
K	yellow-orange-red	
M	red	**coolest**

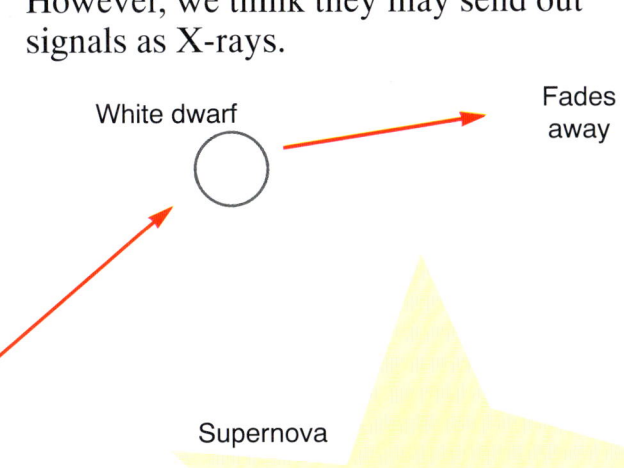

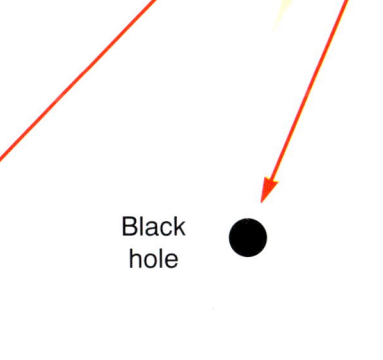

▲ Not all stars have the same life cycle. Some just fade away, but others can end up as pulsars or black holes.

Throughout the universe there are stars at different stages in their lives, rather like the trees in a forest. Some are newly born, others are fully fledged, some are dying. By observing these stars, astronomers have worked out the star life cycle, just as observing trees of different ages in a forest allows us to see the different stages in the life cycle of trees.

The reddish star, Betelgeuse, in Orion is getting old and very large. Already, the whole of the Earth's orbit (93 million miles in radius) could fit inside. When the first human-like creatures were on Earth, Betelgeuse was probably white, far hotter and a lot smaller.

Our star, the Sun, still has a lifetime of about 10,000 million years. Considering that the first microscopic organisms appeared on Earth about 3,800 million years ago and modern humans only 100,000 years ago, we have no reason to worry about our Sun running out of energy.

TIMELINE OF ADVANCE

Here are some of the people, discoveries, inventions and improvements that have brought about our knowledge of the universe today.

Ptolemy An astronomer and geographer (about AD 90–168) who was born in Egypt and worked in the city of Alexandria. He wrote a revolutionary astronomy encyclopaedia known as the *Almagest* which put the Earth at the centre of the universe. It included detailed tables showing the motion of the moon and the Sun and predictions of eclipses.

Ancient Chinese These people made careful records of events occuring in the skies. They recorded Halley's comet and a supernova in AD 1006.

Nicolaus Copernicus A Polish astronomer and clergyman (1473–1523). He proposed a simpler model than Ptolemy for the solar system with the planets, and most important of all the Earth, orbiting the Sun.

Simon Marius A German astronomer (1570–1624) who discovered the four largest moons of Jupiter independently from Galileo in 1610.

Galileo Galilei An Italian astronomer and physicist (1564–1642) who is one of the founders of modern science, his important discoveries and support of the Copernican model for the solar system brought him into conflict with the Roman Catholic Church.

Christian Huygens A Dutch physicist (1629–1693) who discovered the rings around Saturn and its fourth moon in 1655.

Issac Newton An important English scientist (1642–1726) who put forward the theory of gravitation. He also invented a reflecting telescope and proposed three laws of motion that are still used today despite the modern theories of Albert Einstein.

▲ A sixteenth-century picture of Ptolemy using a quadrant to measure the stars.

Edmond Halley A British astronomer and scientist (1656–1742) who worked with Newton at Cambridge and studied comets in detail. He deduced the pattern of appearance of one comet which is now named after him. He was also one of the first people to catalogue the stars of the southern hemisphere.

William Herschel (1732–1822) and **Caroline Herschel**, his sister (1750–1848) were born in Germany. After moving to England they made important discoveries using telescopes they had built themselves. In 1751, William Herschel predicted that other galaxies exist beyond the Milky Way. In 1781, they discovered Uranus. Later they catalogued nebulas and double stars and discovered moons orbiting Uranus and Saturn.

Wilhelm Conrad von Röntgen A German physicist (1845–1923) who, in 1895, discovered the existence of X-rays.

Clyde Tombaugh An American astronomer (1906–) who discovered the planet Pluto in 1930.

Albert Einstein One of the most important scientists (1879–1955) of

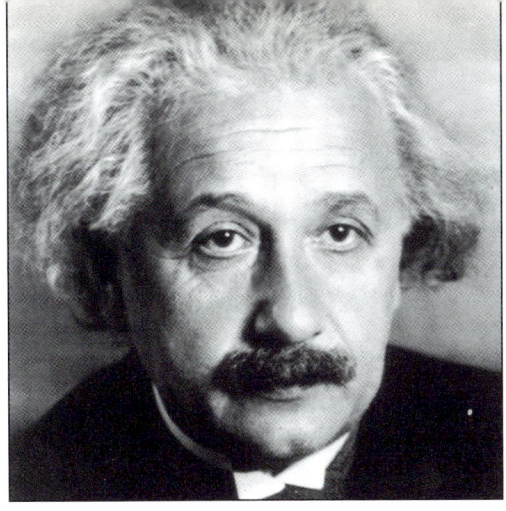

▲ **Albert Einstein photographed in the early 1930s.**

the twentieth century. He was born in Germany but later became first a Swiss and later an American citizen. Not outstanding whilst at school, his theoretical work later helped physicists to understand the nuclear reactions which occur in stars and explain why nothing seemed to travel faster than the speed of light.

Edwin Hubble An American astronomer (1889–1953) who worked at the Mount Wilson Observatory from 1919. He proved that there were more galaxies beyond the Milky Way and showed that they were moving away from us, confirming the idea that the universe is expanding.

Robert Goddard An American rocket pioneer (1882–1945) who fired his first liquid-fuelled rocket on 16 March 1926. It rose 12.5 metres into the air. In 1962 NASA named the Goddard Space Flight Centre, Maryland, USA to honour his work.

Wernher von Braun A German scientist (1912–1977) who designed the first long-distance rocket, providing the basis of all future rocket work. Developed the V2 rockets with which the Germans bombarded London in 1942. After the Second World War, he joined the American rocket-building teams which eventually led to the building of the giant Saturn V rocket.

Major Yuri Gagarin A Russian test pilot who became the first man to travel in space on 12 April 1961.

Valentina Tereshkova A Russian astronaut who becaome the first woman in space on 16 June 1963.

Apollo 11 The US space mission that put astronauts Neil Armstrong and Buzz Aldrin on the surface of the moon for the first time on 21 July 1969.

Voyager 1 and 2 Two space probes launched in 1977 on paths that would take them close to four of the five outer planets. They obtained spectacular pictures of Jupiter, Saturn, Uranus and Neptune and sent back huge amounts of data about the moons, ring systems and gaseous nature of these giant planets. Voyager 2 headed out of the solar system in 1989 carrying messages from Earth.

Space Shuttle Columbia The first of the space shuttle fleet, *Columbia* was first launched in April 1981. Space shuttles are a combination of rocket and glider and are re-usable. Each shuttle is covered with tiles that protect it during re-entry.

Bruce McCandless An American astronaut who was the first human to walk independently in space on 3 February 1984.

Space Shuttle Challenger The worst space disaster to date occurred on 28 January 1986. Space Shuttle *Challenger* exploded at 14,330 metres seventy-three seconds after take-off killing all seven members of the crew.

Mir space station Launched by the Russians in 1986, it has proved a successful orbiting laboratory. It is visited by successive teams of astronauts who spend varying periods of time there. Visited by Britain's first astronaut, Helen Sharman, for eight days in May 1991.

Hubble space telescope Launched from the Shuttle Discovery on 24 April 1990, it was serviced in orbit in December 1993. It was given a new camera, new solar panels, new stabilizing equipment and a corrective optics package. This required five sessions of extravehicular activity each with two astronauts.

Valeri Polyakov A Russian astronaut who returned from the Mir space station in 1995 after setting a new endurance record by spending 438 days in space – longer than any other astronaut up to that time.

GLOSSARY/1

A ready-reference guide to many of the terms used in this book.

Artificial satellite An object launched by a rocket from Earth to orbit a large body in space such as Earth, another planet or a moon.

Asteroids Lumps of rocky material of different sizes that orbit the Sun. Mostly they are found between Mars and Jupiter.

Astrologers People who claim that they can predict events on Earth by studying the movement of the stars and planets.

Atmosphere The blanket of gas surrounding a planet.

Axis The imaginary line through the centre of a globe or sphere. For example the Earth's axis is from the North to the South Pole.

Big bang A massive explosion, about 20 billion years ago, which many scientists believe formed the universe.

Black hole A place in the universe where gravity is so strong that nothing can escape its pull, not even light.

Comet A mixture of rocks and ice that orbits the Sun. When a comet comes near to the Sun the heat produces a glowing tail.

Constellation A pattern that people can see in the stars if they use their imagination. For example the Great Bear.

Convection Convection occurs in a gas or liquid because of gravity. Hotter, less dense material rises and cooler, more dense material falls. Convection occurs in many different ways on Earth. In water it happens as warm water rises and cool water falls. In the air it is vital for keeping us alive – even in a stuffy room there is some convection. It does not happen naturally in an orbiting spacecraft.

Corona The halo of hot dust and gas around the Sun that can be seen during a total eclipse.

Crater A dent or depression in the surface of a moon or planet made by the impact of an object colliding at high speed.

Eclipse An eclipse of the Sun occurs when the moon casts a shadow on the Earth. An eclipse of the moon occurs when the Earth throws a shadow on to the moon.

Ellipse The curved shape, like a squashed circle, of a planet's orbit.

▼ **This is an artist's impression of a black hole. As matter is drawn into the black hole it becomes very hot and glows with light.**

▲ Gliders use rising convection currents in the air to give them lift.

Exosphere The last layer of the atmosphere before 500 kilometres.

Friction The resistance when two things move across each other in different directions.

Galaxy A collection of stars. Some galaxies have several million stars, others have thousands of millions.

Gaia hypothesis The idea that the physical and chemical conditions of the Earth, the atmosphere and the oceans has been and is actively made fit and comfortable by the presence of life on Earth. The Earth's living matter (plants and animals), air, oceans and land together form a complex system which is like a single living thing.

Gravity The pulling force between two objects. You notice it only when one of the objects is massive, like the Earth or Sun.

Greenhouse Effect This is the 'trapping' of the Sun's rays in the Earth's (or any other planet's) atmosphere. The greenhouse gases, mostly carbon dioxide, help to keep the Earth warm but if the greenhouse effect becomes too strong then we may suffer 'global warming' which could have disastrous effects on our planet.

Infra-red One of the waves or rays in the electromagnetic spectrum. It is just outside the visible range and has a slightly longer wavelength than visible light.

Light-year The distance travelled by a ray of light in one year, which is 9.5 million million kilometres.

Local group The collection of about thirty galaxies that includes our own Milky Way. The largest member of the group is the Andromeda galaxy.

Month A lunar month (about twenty-eight days) is the time taken for the moon to travel once round the Earth.

Milky Way The galaxy to which our solar system belongs. It is a spiral-shaped galaxy with about 100,000 stars.

GLOSSARY/2

Nuclear reaction There are two types of nuclear reaction, and both produce tremendous amounts of energy. Fission is the splitting of the centre, or nucleus, of large atoms such as uranium; fusion is the forcing together of smaller atoms, such as hydrogen. Fission is used in the atomic bomb and in generating nuclear power; fusion was used in the hydrogen bomb and is the source of energy in the Sun and other stars.

Nebula This is a large cloud of dust or gas, or a mixture of both, which is the birthplace of stars.

Orbit This is the curved path that a satellite follows around a planet or a planet follows around the Sun.

Ozone A rare compound that has three oxygen atoms joined together instead of the two atoms found in oxygen. In the air near to the ground, it forms only one part in 30 million, but up in the ozone layer it is present in five parts per million. The ozone layer absorbs radiation from the Sun that would be harmful to us if it ever reached the surface of the Earth.

Prominences Huge bursts of burning hydrogen gas which shoot out thousands of kilometres into space from the surface of the sun.

Pulsar A distant star that sends out radio waves in short pulses.

Radiation Energy that is sent out in waves.

Red giant A star that is growing old. As it does so it gets bigger and becomes red in colour.

▲ Nuclear reactions release enormous amounts of energy. If this energy could be safely harnessed it would be of great benefit. Unfortunately, very harmful radiation is also given off which makes the handling of nuclear materials hazardous.

Remote sensing Gathering information from some distance away. For example, collecting information about the Earth using a survey satellite such as LANDSAT or SPOT.

Satellite An object that orbits round another one. For example the moon around the Earth.

Shooting star This is not a star, but a streak of light seen when a small lump of rock, or meteor, burns up as it rushes into the Earth's atmosphere from space.

Space probe A robotic vehicle sent out into space to explore distant planets or other bodies. It uses cameras and other instruments which are controlled from Earth.

Star A giant ball of gas giving out light, heat and other rays.

Stratosphere The layer of the atmosphere above the troposphere which extends from around 50 km above the Earth's surface. The ozone layer occurs in the stratosphere.

Sunspot A cool, dark patch on the Sun's surface.

Supernova The massive explosion of light and heat that occurs at the death of some stars when their nuclear fuel is spent.

Thrust The pushing force of a rocket measured in newtons.

Troposphere The layer of the atmosphere closest to the Earth's surface. It rises 8 kilometres over the poles and 16–17 kilometres over the Equator. It is the region which contains the life on Earth and in which all the weather occurs.

Ultraviolet One of the waves or rays in the electromagnetic spectrum, just outside the visible range because it has a wavelength slightly shorter than visible light.

Year The time taken for the Earth to orbit the Sun once.

GOING FURTHER

Books There are a large number of books on space. Here is a selection:
Earth in Space by Robert Stephenson and Roger Browne, Wayland 1991
Galileo by Douglas McTavish, Wayland 1991
Our Universe by Terry Jennings, Wayland 1989
Planet Earth and the Universe by Duncan Brewer, Cherrytree 1992
Space Travel by Robin Kerrod, Wayland 1991
The Super Science Book of Space by Jerry Wellington, Wayland 1993
The Big Book of Stars and Planets by Robin Kerrod, Octopus 1990
The Inner Planets by Neil Ardley, Heinemann 1991
The Kingfisher Facts and Records Book of Space by Stuart Atkinson, Kingfisher 1990
The Outer Planets by Neil Ardley, Heinemann 1991
The Usborne Book of Space Facts by Struan Reid, Usborne, 1987

Places to visit Places in Britain include:
Jodrell Bank Science Centre, Macclesfield, Cheshire SK11 9DL – an interactive science centre, attached to the famous research centre which pioneered radio astronomy, with its own planetarium.
The London Planetarium, Marylebone Road, London NW1 5LR – world famous since it opened in 1958.
Stardome: the Travelling Planetarium – this travels to you; it is a portable, inflatable planetarium for 20–25 people which can be rented by groups, schools or colleges (contact: Dennis Ashton, Sheffield Hallam University, S10 2BP).

CD-ROM/Multimedia
Earth and Universe, BTL Publishing, Bradford BD7 1BX
The Interactive Space Encyclopaedia presented by Patrick Moore, Andromeda Interactive, Abingdon OX14 3PX
Redshift, Maris Multimedia, London E1 8AX

INDEX

Numbers in **bold** refer to pictures or drawings as well as text.

Afanasyef, Viktor 29
Aldrin, Buzz **20**
Apollo programme 20
    Apollo 11 20, 43
Armstrong, Neil **20**, 21
Arrest, Heinrich d' 25
Artsebarski, Anatoli **28**
asteroids 27, 44
astronaut 18, 19, **20**, **21**, **28**, **29**, 30, 31, **32-33**, 34, 35
atmosphere 4, 5, 15, 19, 21, 22, 31, 37, 44
    clouds **4**, 21, **22**
    layers **4**
    ozone 4, 5, 46

Baker, Michael **34**
Bell, Jocelyn 37
big bang theory **7**, 44
black hole **41**, **44**
Braun, Wernher von 18, 43

Christy, James 25
Collins, Michael **20**
comet 26, 27, 44
    Halley **26**
    Shoemaker-Levy **26**
constellations 10, 44
Copernicus, Nicolaus **6**, **7**, 42
Couch Adams, John 25

eclipse **13**, 44
Einstein, Albert 9, 42, **43**
electromagnetic spectrum **16**
EVA **31**

Friedmann, Alexandra 7

Gagarin, Yuri 30, 43
    survival rations **30**

Gaia hypothesis 36, 45
galaxies 7, 9, **11**, 45
    Andromeda **11**
    Milky Way 11, 45
Galilei, Galileo 7, 12, 42
Galle, Johann 25
geostationary orbit **17**
g-force 29
Goddard, Robert 18, 43
gravity 9, 18, 20, 21, 25, 31, 36, 40, 45

Halley, Edmond 26, 42
Helvius, Johannes, 23
Herschel, William 25, 42
Hillary, Edmund 5
Himalayas **5**
Hubble, Edwin 43
Huygens, Christian 25, 42

Juno mission 28

Kirkalev, Sergei **28**, 29

Lee, Mark **31**
Lemaître, Georges 7
Le Verrier, Urbain 25
Leonov, Alexei **28**, 43
lifeforms 38, **39**
Lovelock, James 36
Low, David **31**

Manarov, Musa 29
Marius, Simon 8, 42
McCandless, Bruce 43
meteor 27
meteorite **27**
    Barringer Crater **27**
moon 4, **8-9**, 14, **14-15**, 15, 18, 20, **21**, 23, 25, 26, 27, 36
    Charon 15
    Io **8**

NASA 18, **32-33**, 35
Newton, Isaac 7, 8, **9**, 42
nuclear reaction 40, **46**

observatories 37
    Mount Stromlo 26
    Puklova 37

planets 4, 5, **6**, **7**, 8, 9, 22, 23, 24, 25, 26, 38, 39
    Earth 4, 5, **6**, **7**, 8, 9, 13, 14, 16, **17**, 18, 19, 20, 21, 22, 23, 26, 27, 29, 30, 31, **35**, **36**, 37, 38, 39, 41
    Jupiter **6**, **7** 8, **24**, **26**, 27
    Mars **6**, **7**, 22, **23**, 24, 27, **38**
    Mercury **6**, **7**, **22-23**
    Neptune 19, 24, **25**
    Pluto 15, 24, **25**
    Saturn **6**, **7**, 19, 24, **25**
    Uranus 19, 24, **25**
    Venus **6**, **7**, **22**, 23
Polyakov, Valeri 43
Ptolemy **6**, 42
pulsars 37, **41**, 46

Riccioli, Giovanni 14
rockets 18, 19, 29
    Saturn V **18**, **20**
Röntgen, Wilhelm 16, 42

satellite 16, 17, 19, 44, 46
    INTELSAT **17**
    NOAA **17**
    SEASTAR 37
    SPUTNIK 16
Sharman, Helen **28**, 29
shooting stars 27, 46
sky 4. 8, 10, 11, 14, 18, 22, 27, 37, 39
solar system 7, 9, 15, 24, 25, 26, 27, 39
space food **34**, 35
space shuttle **18-19**, **32-33**
    Challenger 43
    Columbia 19, 31, 43
    Discovery **36-37**

space station 19, **35**
    Mir 19, **28-29**, 43
space suit **21**
space toilet 35
spacecraft 19, 20, 29, 39
    Magellan **22**
    Mariner **23**
    Pioneer **24**
    Soyuz **28**, **29**
    Viking 23
    Vostok 30
    Voyager **19**, 24, 25, **38**, 39, 43
stars **8-9**, **10**, **11**, 19, **40-41**, 46
    blue giant 40
    life cycle **40-41**
    nebula **40**, 46
    red dwarf 40
    red giant **40**, 46
    supernova 40, **41**, 46
    white dwarf 40, **41**
Sun 5, 8, 9, **12-13**, 21, 22, 23, 27, 36, 39, 40, 41
    sunspots 8, **12**, 46

telescope 7, 8, **9**, 12, 14, 25, 26, 37, 39
    Hubble **36-37**, 43
    Newton **9**
    radio 37, 39
    X-ray 39
Tenzing Norgay 5
Tereshkova, Valentina 43
Tombaugh, Clyde 25, 42

UFO 38
universe 4, **6**, **7**, 30, 38, 39, 41

weightlessness 29, **32-33**

X-ray **16**, 41

Young, John **32-33**

48